It's Just Poetry

Mia Whitehead

Presentation by *BookLeaf Publishing*

Web: www.bookleafpub.com

E-mail: info@bookleafpub.com

ISBN: 9789360942571

First edition 2024

*I dedicate this book to my kids because I
want them to know that anything is possible
when you set your mind to it. That patience
is key.*

ACKNOWLEDGEMENT

I would like to send a special thank you to my boyfriend for believing in me and pushing me to do this. I truly appreciate your support.

False Reality

Somewhere down the line I lost myself,
I lost myself in a false reality. The false reality
of the little spark that flickered would light the
flame again. When ultimately it has suddenly
died. I lost myself in a false reality, thinking that
one day you'd change the way you treated me.
That you'd realize the love I gave defeated me.
Yet, I still held on to that flicker I didn't want to
die. Coming out of this false reality, i realized
that in actually you're not the one for me. That
life goes on with or without you I just have to
find my peace. Even if that means leaving my
false reality to come back to face true reality. So
I may let go.

Will You Allow Me?

Will you allow me to love you for a lifetime?
Will you allow me to love you with your flaws
and all?
Will you allow me to love you through your
mental, physical, emotional, and spiritual wars?
Will you allow me to love you when you over
think?
Will you allow me to love you through the silent
cries you hide?
Will you allow me to love you through a kiss?
Through a hug? Through the touch of our
hands?
Will you allow me to love you in your
vulnerability?
Will you allow me to love the little boy deep
down who may not have felt love before?
Will you allow me to love you beyond your
pain?
Will you allow me to love you through the
good? The bad? The ugly?
Will you allow me to love your soul? Mind?
Body? Spirit?
Will you allow me to love you for a lifetime?
And ever after?

Special Kind

You are a special kind, a special kind that is rare to find. You're like a rose growing through concrete, you will blossom and shine. Through the rain and stormy weather you keep on pushing and keep your head up and continue to rise. Yet broken mentally, physically, and emotionally you have the purest heart that is hard to find. You, my friend, are a special kind.

Behind the Mask

Behind the mask, hidden from view, lies a person yearning to break free.
With every layer stripped away, the true self emerges to play. And with every layer peeled back, comes a newfound sense of freedom. No longer bound by societal norms or expectations, the true self shines brighter than ever before. With each layer gone, the true self emerges, strong and pure. No longer hiding in fear, but standing proud and secure. To reveal thy true self from behind the mask.

Nature's Peace of Mind

In the silence of the forest, where leaves rustle and birds sing sweetly, I find solace and tranquility, my soul at ease. The sunlight filters through the branches overhead, casting a dappled pattern on the ground below. The breeze whispers secrets through the trees, carrying the scent of wildflowers. As I inhale deeply to exhale and breathe.

Strength of a Sunflower

The sunflower stands tall and proud, its petals following the sun's path across the sky. Its beauty lies in its simplicity
- bright yellow petals surrounding a brilliant center. The sunflower is a symbol of strength and resilience, bending with the wind yet standing firm in its
convictions. Its radiance illuminates the earth with a warmth that penetrates deeply into the soul.

A Silent Love

In whispers soft, I once declared
My love for you, no mask, no facade.
Each day, like sacred hymn, I'd say,
"I love you," in the sweetest way.
But now, a silence fills the air,
The words I held, I cannot bear.
For in my heart, a wrenching ache,
To see those words, I dare not break.
It hurts to keep this love concealed,
To bury what once was revealed.
Yet fear and doubt, they grip so tight,
They shroud my love in darkest night.
Oh, how I long to set it free,
To say those words, to let them be.
But until then, I'll hold them near,
In whispered hopes, you'll always hear.
So though I may not speak the phrase,
Know that my love still brightly blaze.
And in the quiet of our days,
I'll love you in a million ways.

Unconditional Love

In the heart's deep chamber, a flame does burn,
A love that flows, with no concern.
It knows no bounds, no limit to its grace,
A tender embrace in every space.
It's the gentle touch in times of need,
A soothing balm, a sacred creed.
Through highs and lows, it stands tall,
Unconditional love, the greatest of all.
In moments of joy, it sings its song,
And in sorrow's depths, it keeps us strong.
It's the light that guides, in darkest night,
A beacon of hope, forever bright.
Not bound by rules, nor by time's decree,
It flows endlessly, pure and free.
In every smile, every tear shed,
Unconditional love, forever spread.
So let it be our guiding star,
No matter where we roam or how far.
For in its warmth, we find our home,
Unconditional love, forever known.

Special

In moments rare, a bond so true,
A feeling deep, forever grew.
A cherished connection, none can displace,
In each other's hearts, a special space.
Amid life's journey, twists and turns,
A special light within us burns.
Guiding us through both joy and strife,
A beacon of hope in this dance of life.
Through laughter shared and tears that fall,
Special memories weave a cherished thrall.
In the tapestry of time, they gleam,
A testament to love's eternal dream.
So let us treasure what's unique,
Embrace the magic that we seek.
For in the ordinary and the grand,
Lies the special touch of life's sweet hand.

Lost in Nature

In the heart of the wild, I roam,
Nature's embrace becomes my home.
Lost in its beauty, I'm set free,
A love affair with land and sea.
Beneath the azure sky so wide,
I wander where the rivers glide.
Among the trees, a tranquil trance,
Lost in nature's sweet romance.
Whispers of leaves, a gentle breeze,
Nature's symphony puts my soul at ease.
Mountains tall and valleys low,
In this world, I find my flow.
A tapestry of colors, rich and bright,
Dancing with the day's soft light.
I'm but a wanderer, no longer lost,
In nature's love, I've paid the cost.

Growth

In the shadow's grip, anger flares,
Hurt and pain, no one shares.
Beneath the weight, I bend and sway,
Lost in darkness, day by day.
But seeds of change within me sow,
Slowly, roots of strength start to grow.
Through cracks of doubt, light filters in,
Hope whispers softly, I begin.
With each step forward, wounds may heal,
The past's sharp edges start to peel.
Forgiveness blooms, a gentle flower,
Empowering me with newfound power.
Through trials faced and lessons learned,
From the fire's burn, wisdom earned.
Rising above, I spread my wings,
In joy and gratitude, my heart sings.
Transformed, uplifted, I soar high,
Beneath the vast and endless sky.
From anger to joy, my journey's told,
Personal growth, a story bold.

Self-Love

12

Embrace the skin you're in, Give yourself
permission to grin,
Acknowledge the victories won,
And learn from mistakes that have been undone.
Be patient with your shortcomings,
Forgive yourself for your wrongdoings,
Remember kindness is a virtue,
And recognize the beauty within you.

Vulnerability

In shadows deep, where fears abide,
A soul cries out, no place to hide.
Seeking solace, seeking light,
Through darkest valleys of the night.
In whispered echoes, voices call,
Yet silence reigns, a heavy pall.
But courage blooms, a fragile seed,
To take the step, to plant the need.
Through winding paths of heart and mind,
A journey taken, hope to find.
In therapists' rooms, a sacred space,
Where truths are spoken, fears embrace.
With gentle hands and empathetic eyes,
The healer listens, no disguise.
Through tears and laughter, pain revealed,
A wounded heart begins to heal.
So seek the help, don't walk alone,
For in vulnerability, strength is grown.
In seeking aid, we find our power,
To face the storm, to seize the hour.
For mental health is not a flaw,
But a journey, a sacred law.
So let us walk, hand in hand,
Towards the light, towards the land
Of healing, hope, and understanding,
Where broken souls find sweet remanding.

Single Mother

In the quiet of the night, when stars softly gleam,
There walks a woman, her strength a silent
stream.
A single mother, brave and true,
Her love, a beacon, guiding her through.
With hands that toil and eyes that weep,
She nurtures dreams, her children keep.
Through trials and triumphs, she stands tall,
A warrior heart, through it all.
In the warmth of her embrace, worries fade
away,
For in her love, there's solace every day.
She bears the burdens, carries the load,
With grace and courage, down life's winding
road.
Through laughter and tears, she finds her way,
With resilience and hope, she greets each day.
Her love knows no bounds, her strength
profound,
A single mother, forever crowned.
So here's to the single mothers, brave and true,
Your love and sacrifice, we honor you.
In your embrace, we find our home,
For your love, dear mother, forever roams.

A Father's Embrace

In the heart of every child, a bond so deep,
With a father's love, their dreams take flight and
leap.
Through laughter and tears, in moments big and
small,
A father's presence, the greatest gift of all.
With steady hands and a guiding light,
He teaches, he nurtures, through day and night.
In his embrace, fears melt away,
For in his love, there's strength to stay.
With each step taken, his hand to hold,
In his wisdom, a story unfolds.
He's the hero in their childhood tale,
With every challenge, he helps them prevail.
Through triumphs and setbacks, he's always
there,
With unwavering love, beyond compare.
In his laughter, they find joy anew,
For in his presence, their hearts renew.
So here's to the fathers, steadfast and true,
Your love and guidance, we honor you.
In your arms, we find our home,
For your love, dear father, forever roams.

Harmony's Embrace

In the rhythm's embrace, I find my way,
Lost in melodies that gently sway.
With each note played, my soul takes flight,
In the symphony of day and night.
The bassline pulses, a heartbeat strong,
Guiding me through where I belong.
In the lyrics sung, stories unfold,
A tapestry of emotions, pure and bold.
With every chord struck, I drift away,
In the harmonies, I find my stay.
The world fades out, and I'm entranced,
In the sanctuary of music, I dance.
With each crescendo, a surge of emotion,
A symphony of life in perpetual motion.
Lost in the melody, I am free,
In the rhythm's embrace, eternally.
So let the music carry me away,
In its embrace, I'll forever stay.
For in its depths, I find my muse,
Lost in the music, I refuse to lose.

Black Sheep

In the fold of kin, a lone black sheep,
Wanders amidst the flock, secrets to keep.
Different hues, a contrast stark,
In the family portrait, a distinct mark.
Misunderstood, yet fiercely free,
A rebel soul, wild and untamed, you see.
Straying from the path, carving your own way,
In the shadowed corners, you choose to stay.
Unruly heart, with dreams unfurled,
In the tapestry of tradition, an outlier in the
world.
Yet beneath the surface, a fire burns bright,
A spirit unbroken, a guiding light.
Though judged by some, you stand tall and true,
For authenticity, your guiding virtue.
In your uniqueness, strength resides,
A beacon of defiance against conformity's tides.
Embrace your difference, let your voice be
heard,
For in your uniqueness, lies your power,
undeterred.
Black sheep of the family, shine on with pride,
For in your own way, you're destined to glide.

There's Light at the End

In the shadows, I quietly sway,
Life's storms sweep me far away.
Families clash, and I'm left astray,
Lost in the night, where dreams decay.
Each blow a burden, too heavy to bear,
In the depths of despair, I find solace there.
But hope flickers, a dim, distant flare,
Guiding me through this relentless despair.
Though battered and bruised, I rise once more,
With resilience in my core, I begin to explore.
For even in darkness, there's a path to restore,
To find peace within, and open new doors.

A Flicker of Hope

In shadows deep, where darkness thrives,
A flicker stirs, where hope survives.
Through trials dire, and tempests wild,
It whispers softly, like a child.
In hearts weighed down by sorrow's plight,
It sparkles on through darkest night.
With every tear that's shed in woe,
It plants a seed, a light to grow.
When storms rage fierce, and doubts assail,
It's steadfast, like a ship's strong sail.
Through valleys low and mountains high,
It guides us on, towards the sky.
So let us cherish, guard, and tend,
This flame of hope, that has no end.
For in its glow, we find our way,
And keep the darkness at bay.

Strength and Grace

In times of struggle and pain, you stand tall,
Exhausted yet resilient, you give it your all.
Through moments heavy with despair and woe,
You find the strength to keep on the go.
With a heart that's pure and tull of grace, You
navigate life's challenges with poise and grace.
In moments light, your spirit shines bright,
Bringing joy and laughter, a guiding light.
So here's to you, strong and true,
May your days be filled with love and
breakthroughs.
Remember to breathe, take breaks when needed,
For in your journey, you are always succeeded.

The Journey to Everlasting Joy

In shadows deep, where trials reign,
A heart once burdened, filled with pain.
Yet through the storm, a light did gleam,
A spark of hope, a distant dream.
Through valleys low and mountains high,
With every tear, a whispered sigh.
But steadfast stood the weary soul,
With courage strong, to reach the goal.
And as the dawn breaks, bright and clear,
The clouds disperse, the path draws near.
For in the end, through strife and test,
Comes sweet reward, a peaceful rest.
The happily ever after, at last,
For one who struggled, but held fast.
A tale of triumph, of love untold,
Where dreams take flight, and hearts unfold.